Sevilla

The Glory of the Guadalquivir

susaeta

Popular architecture characterised by its window grilles and
shady patios are urban marks
left by the Romano-Muslim culture in Seville.

Edited by:
Thema, Equipo Editorial, S.A.

Photography by:
Marc Llimargas

Translated by:
Carole Patton

© SUSAETA EDICIONES, S.A.
Campezo, s/n - 28022 Madrid
Tel. 913 009 100 - Fax 913 009 118

Flower-studded balconies adorn the streets of the *Barrio de Santa Cruz*.

Contents

Seville

The Glory of the Guadalquivir

*"Such adornment and greatness
of streets, I don't know
If Augustus ever saw them in Rome
or had such wealth."*

Lope de Vega («La Estrella de Sevilla»)

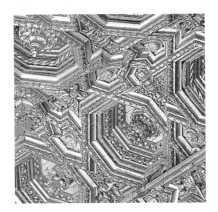

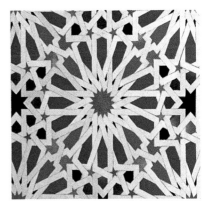

Refinement
Geometrical precision on one of the dining-room walls at the *Reales Alcázares*.

Religiousness
Christian Gothic details on the retable of the High Altar in the Main Chapel.

Beauty
Remarkable stuccoes and marquetrywork at the *Reales Alcázares*.

Magnificence
Almohade ornamentation in the *Patio de las Doncellas* at the *Reales Alcázares*.

Sumptuosity
The Mudéjar design highlights the opulence of the courtyard at *Pilate's House*.

Harmony
Equilibrium prevails throughout the *Moorish Kings' Bedroom* at the *Reales Alcázares*.

La Maestranza bullring seen from the banks of the Guadalquivir.

Seville

The Glory of the Guadalquivir

THE ORIGINS OF HISPALIS
Work of Hercules

Seville, the capital of the Autonomous Community of Andalusia, is a lively, beautiful and modern city, the fourth most-inhabited in Spain. A thousand years young, built on the banks of the River Guadalquivir, it was once one of the wealthiest and busiest cities in Europe, where trade with the New World was centralised, incredible shipments of gold and silver being brought into its harbour.

Like any mythical city, the origins of Seville are a mixture of history and legend. The more imaginative scholars say it was founded by Hercules, who gave it to his son Hispalus, from where

Flamenco Guitar

Sevillians pay homage to the instrument which best conveys their feelings, beside *Triana* bridge.

Plaza de España

Separated from the Park of *María Luisa* by the *Avenida de Isabel la Católica*, the *Plaza de España* is an arcaded area of Neo-classical columns and tiled walls depicting historical events of the different provinces of Spain.

Walls

There used to be about 6 kilometres of walls in the 16th century, with wide parapet walks, numerous towers and gates, many of which were later restored, and battlemented barbicans.

Sevillian House

The Romano-Muslim style became a characteristic of Sevillian houses, which maintained their brightly-coloured façades and balconies.

its name comes; others identify it with the biblical Tarsis, the city of metals with which King Solomon traded or where Jonah wanted to flee before being swallowed by the whale.

Those who prefer an historical explanation believe that it has its origins in *Ispal*, a settlement founded by the Iberian tribe of the Turdetans, descendents of the Tartessians, around the 8th century B.C. An example of the splendour of those days could be the fabulous Tartessian treasure of *El Carambolo* which was discovered in 1959 near the popular district of *Triana*, a replica of which is on display at the *Archaeological Museum*.

Strategically located on the banks of the River Guadalquivir, the ancient settlement soon be-

came an important centre of trade which attracted Greek, Phoenician and Carthaginian merchants, who would go up the river from where Sanlúcar de Barrameda is situated today. The Carthaginians fortified it during the Punic Wars between Carthage and Rome, but this did not prevent the Roman legions from conquering and destroying it in 205 B.C.

Under the Romanised name of *Hispalis*, the township was rebuilt and suffered the civil conflicts of Rome until Julius Caesar made it into the assize town of *Iulia Romula Hispalis* in 43 B.C. This is how the city standing on the banks of the *Baetis*, name given by the Romans to the Guadalquivir, became very prosperous. A few years later,

Islamic Wrought Iron
Christian blacksmiths inherited the forging skills from the Muslims and carried on their tradition, as we can see in this splendid wrought-iron detail on the *Puerta del Perdón* of Seville Cathedral.

The Tower of Gold
This emblematic monument built by the Almohades in the early 13th century to defend the harbour from Christian attacks, used to be covered with golden tiles.

Augustus granted it the privilege of coining money, and its increasing importance could be measured by the size of the walls enclosing the town, its sewer system and the magnificence of its citizens. Although a rival in the control of trade with Rome to nearby *Itálica*, today Santiponce, the birthplace of the emperors Trajan and Hadrian, the Christianisation of the Empire consolidated its position by naming it the seat of the first episcopate of the province of *Baetica*.

During the decline of the Roman Empire, the city was occupied and plundered by Siling Vandals in 411, but 18 years later they were driven out by the Visigoths, who turned it into the capital of their kingdom. As a capital, it witnessed religious confrontation between Arians and Christians, which, to a certain extent, concealed a secret fight for power between aristocratic Visigoth families. An example of these strained relations was the rising of the Christian Hermenigild against his father, the Arian Leovigild, in 573. After the latter had besieged the city by diverting the course of the river, he attacked it and killed his rebel son. From that moment on, the Visigothic court left Seville, but the city still remained a centre of culture thanks to its bishops Leandro, who managed to convert Reccared to Christianity at the Council of Toledo, 589, and Isidore, the author of *Etymologiae*, a vast encyclopaedia of learning of the age.

Ishbiliya, the Muslim Splendour

In 711, after the defeat of the last Visigothic king, Roderic, at the Battle of Guadalete, the Arabs took control of the city, renaming it *Ishbiliya*, pronounced *shbilya* by the people, from where *Sevilla* comes. Arab dominion magnified the urban landscape of Seville, giving it some of its most beautiful and emblematic monuments, such as the *Giralda* Tower and the *Torre del Oro*.

First seat of the court of emir Abd al-Aziz, Seville soon rivalled Cordoba for being the largest and most important city of the peninsula. As head of the Caliphate, Cordoba still remained the most important, although Seville continued being

The Christ of Triana
This is one of the most beautiful images of Christ which is taken out in procession during Holy Week by approximately 50 brotherhoods of the city.

Holy Week
Easter processions in Seville are full of religious piety, reaching their maximum point of expression in the *Madrugá* procession which takes place between Maundy Thursday and Good Friday.

a renowned city of *Al-Andalus*, not reaching its splendour until the Caliphate of Cordoba fell in 1013, when it became the head of an independent kingdom. Specially prosperous were the reigns of Al-Mutamid, learned monarch and poet, who ruled from 1069 to 1090, and those of the Almohade monarchs. During the rule of the Almohade dynasty, between the 12th and 13th centuries, the city of Seville grew so much that it went beyond the defensive walls and reached the other bank of the *Wadi el Kebir* ("the great river" in Arabic), where populous neighbourhoods were formed, such as *Triana*.

At the same time, the city was embellished with splendid buildings, such as the *Alcázar* and the great mosque, of which is left its minaret known today as *La Giralda* and the *Patio de los Naranjos*. The Arabs also carried out defensive works, remains of which are: the *Macarena* walls; gates, for example, *Puerta de Córdoba*; or towers, such as the *Torre del Oro*, which, together with the *Torre de la Plata*, protected the harbour entrance against possible Christian attacks.

Christian Splendour
When King Fernando III conquered Seville in 1248, it meant a milestone in the War of Reconquest undertaken by the Christians in the north of the peninsula. After taking the Almohade capital, the Castilian-Leonese monarch set up court

there, where his son, Alfonso X "The Wise One", would later be crowned. The cosmopolitan character of this great monarch and his true concern about culture, made him establish an important school of Arabic and Latin, which had its correlation in the famous *Toledo School of Translators*, a real centre of dissemination of knowledge accumulated by the Arabs over the centuries.

During the conflict between Alfonso X and his son, Sancho, Seville was the only city that remained loyal to him to the end. This sign of loyalty and the king's profound gratitude became the city's motto, in the form of the letters *NODO* (*No me ha dejado*: "It did not abandon me"), which Alfonso X ordered to be inscribed and carved everywhere.

The control of the Port of Seville was key to the favourable outcome for the Christians in the long war waged against the Muslims. This is why successive Castilian monarchs spent long periods of time in this city, for example Pedro I "The Cruel" and Juan I, the first to reform and enlarge the old, sumptuous *Alcázar* which used to belong to the Almohades.

During the reign of the Catholic Monarchs, the end of the War of Reconquest, and, above all, the discovery, conquest and colonisation of America, determined a new and magnificent age of splendour for Seville, which would become one of the most cosmopolitan and populous cities in Europe.

The Gold from the New World

Between the 16th and 17th centuries, especially during the reigns of Carlos V and Felipe II, Seville lived its days of maximum glory. The "Great

Puerta del Perdón

Flanked by sculptures of the Apostles St. Peter and St. Paul, the *Puerta del Perdón* of the Cathedral is a fine example of Moorish-style adornment, with a double horseshoe arch and doors made of larch covered with bronze, vestiges of the old mosque. Together with the *Puerta del Lagarto*, it leads the way into the *Patio de los Naranjos* ("Courtyard of the Orange Trees").

Christian Saints

Christian Saints made of clay decorate the main façade of Seville Cathedral.

Patio in Triana
Splendid railings and beautiful plants adorn the peaceful patios of Sevillian houses.

Street in Triana
This district located on the right side of the River Guadalquivir and whose name evokes the Roman emperor Trajan, is considered to be the cradle of flamenco music.

Babylon of Spain" was "port and gateway of the New World" in words of the poet Lope de Vega, which would bustle with an intense traffic of goods and precious metals. Few cities compared to Seville in social activity during the so-called Spanish *Golden Age*.

Its streets swarmed with merchants, bankers, tradesmen, public officials, poets, artists, priests and rogues, and were lined with inns, eating houses, hostels and taverns, like the one frequented by Cervantes on *Calle Bayona*, belonging to his friend, Tomás Gutiérrez.

Another part of this multicoloured urban landscape was made up by *corrales*, old playhouses, whose owners would contract companies of comedians, who nearly always performed plays by Sevillian playwrights, for example, Juan de la Cueva, famous for his dramatic works full of simplicity and genuineness, or Lope de Rueda.

So, the hustle and bustle, the smells and the comings and goings of the old Arab market places and silk merchants' districts extended to the arcaded streets where goldsmiths, silversmiths, blacksmiths, potters and other artisans worked, as well as in squares and other open spaces of the city where street markets, fairs and junk dealers were installed.

Starting from the harbour, the city bustled with activity and grew in a frenzied way, beyond the limits of its walls and went from a population of 75,000 inhabitants in 1500 to 150,000 in 1588. Districts were progressively enlarged; new squares and boulevards built; and churches, palaces and mansions erected, giving the city an aspect that corresponded with the wealth and vitality of the new times.

The Dukes of Alba, the Marquises of Tarifa and the Dukes of Medina-Sidonia had sumptuous mansions built, such as the palaces of *Las Dueñas*, *Los Guzmanes* or the so-called *Casa de Pilatos*. At the same time, rich Andalusian, Biscayan, Catalan, Genoese, Florentine, German, Dutch and *indiano* [Spanish emigrants who returned to Spain after making a fortune in Latin America] merchants also had their own splendid mansions and palaces constructed.

Feria de Abril

Soon after Holy Week comes the "April Fair" where Sevillians let their hair down, strolling, dancing, singing, and drinking for several days. This typical celebration has its origins in the agricultural fairs known as *Cincuesma and San Miguel*, established by Alfonso X "The Wise" in 1292. Isabel II gave them a new impulse in 1847 and the inhabitants of Seville set up their stands to attend to farmers and entertain them at night with their singing, heel-tapping and hand-clapping.

Capital of Trade and Centre of the World

The *Casa de Contratación* was built by royal order in 1503 and was the centre from which all trade with America was controlled. During the same period, Seville promoted its university and had the first printing house of the Castilian Crown.

However, from the second half of the 17th century, changes occurred on an international scale, which, together with a series of local factors, meant the end of Seville's age of splendour and the beginning of a long period of decadence.

The landscape and bustling activity of Seville came to a standstill until 1929, when an attempt was made to make up for lost time and become a modern city.

Fernando III

This equestrian statue of the Castilian-Leonese monarch Fernando "The Saint" is situated in the *Plaza Nueva* in front of the Town Hall. This king took Seville from Muslim control on 23rd November 1248, turning it into the seat of his Court and a strategic enclave during the War of Reconquest.

In that year Seville was host to the Ibero-American Exhibition, which, in spite of coinciding with the outbreak of the world-wide Depression, brought important town-planning reforms, such as the *Parque de María Luisa*, today one of the most popular parks frequented by Sevillians.

Seville and the Age of Technology

The Spanish Civil War put an abrupt end to this brief period of modernisation, and the years of dictatorship did not do much to favour the situation. So, after the restoration of democracy and within a framework of profound social and political changes in Spain, Seville found another chance of promoting itself and becoming one of the most modern cities in Europe with the 1992 World Exhibition, dedicated to commemorating the V Centenary of the Discovery of America by Christopher Columbus.

Once it had been named the capital of the Autonomous Community of Andalusia, following the new political-administrative map of democratic Spain, Seville undertook some very important works in order to commemorate the discovery of the New World. The 1992 World Exhibition took place on the *Isla de la Cartuja*, whose monastery founded in 1401 had been turned into a famous ceramics factory in 1839. Apart from the impressive theme pavilions, such as those dedicated to the Discovery, Navigation, Present and Future, as well as those corresponding to each of the countries taking part, the ultramodern *Santa Justa* Railway Station for the *AVE* high-speed train joining Madrid and Seville, and the *Alamillo* Bridge, work of the architect Santiago Calatrava, were also built.

Therefore, now at the beginning of the 21st century, Seville is at the same time a traditional and a modern city. It is a city that has known how to recover its modernity based on a glorious past, during which it became the political, economical and cultural capital of the West.

María Luisa Park

The former gardens of the *Palace of San Telmo* were given to the people of Seville by the *Infanta María Luisa Fernanda de Orleans* in 1893. Designed by Jean Forestier, this park, which was host to the 1929 Ibero-American Exhibition, offers inviting spots where one may relax, such as this one in the *Plaza de América*.

The Giralda Tower

A noble and elegant tower, which the Christians did not dare demolish and that, in time, became the Cathedral bell tower, under the popular name of *Giralda* ("The Weather Vane"). The great Almohade mosque was begun in 1184, during the days of Abu Yuqub Yusuf. Gever Ahmed Ibn Baso and Ali de Gomara were two of the master builders of the mosque who also gave the temple this magnificent rectangular minaret with four golden spheres on the top.

The Giralda Tower

From the top of the Giralda, 94 metres up, there is a fine view of the white houses of Seville and its old monuments. The outside of the tower contrasts greatly with the inside, since the latter has no adornment, consisting of 35 gentle, spiral ramps, illuminated by narrow windows, which go up to the flat roof on the top.

Symbols of perfection and nobleness, the golden spheres fell off during the 1355 earthquake and were replaced by a Christian cross. In 1568, the architect Hernán Ruiz el Mozo added to what was now the Cathedral bell tower four Renaissance-style bodies, which he crowned with a bronze weather vane, work of Bartolomé Morel which represents Faith and is known by the people of Granada as *Giralda* or *Giraldillo* ("the little weather vane"), which gives tne name to this tower.

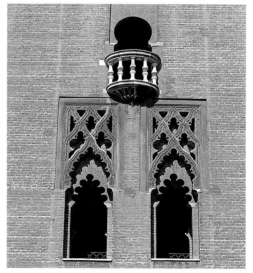

Reales Alcázares

Palace-fortress symbolising the social and political privilege held by Seville for centuries, both for Muslims and for Christians. Its exquisite refinement is not out-of-tune with the military nature of its original construction. Arab sultans and Castilian kings alike found peaceful solace in its patios and gardens, as well as in its luxurious apartments.

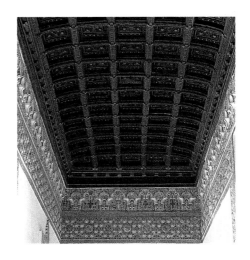

Reales
Alcázares

The Patio de las Doncellas, with its splendid friezes of polychrome tiles, stuccoes and lavishly-adorned arches, is evidence of the original 11th –century *alcázar*.

Al-Mubarak or Palacio de la Bendición was the name given to the palace-fortress by King Al-Mutamid, who ordered its construction on the site of the primitive fortress built by Abd-el-Rahman in the 9th century.

Pedro I "The Cruel", had the *alcázar* rebuilt as a residence in the 14th century, being the main artificer of its current appearance. The Catholic Monarchs and Carlos V, who celebrated his wedding with Isabel I of Portugal here, also added new rooms.

Reales Alcázares

The power and the glory are shown here in the magnificence of tiles and complex stuccowork in rooms such as the *Salón de Carlos V* and the *Salón de los Embajadores*, where Renaissance and *Mudéjar* ornamental motifs harmonise. Therefore, not in vain does the inscription on the façade of the Reales Alcázares read, "The very distinguished, noble, powerful, and conquering King Pedro, ordered the construction of these *alcázares*, palaces and façades...".

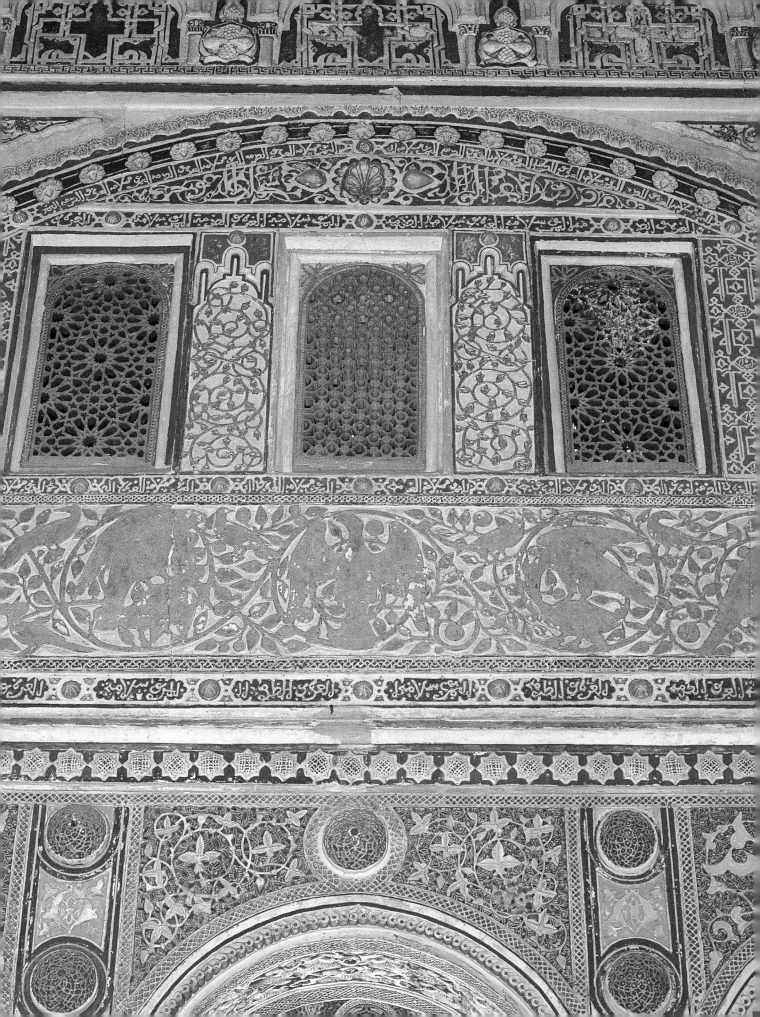

P·E·R·M·E·R·E·G·E·S·R·E·G·N·A·N·T

The Cathedral

Monumental Temple of Christianity. Begun in 1401 on the site of the main mosque, its grandeur can be compared to that of St. Peter's in Rome, St. Paul's in London and the Yamoussoukro on the Ivory Coast. Even so, it is the largest Christian Gothic-Renaissance Cathedral, whose main artificers were Simón de Colonia, Alfonso Rodríguez, Juan Gil de Hontañón, Diego de Riaño and Hernán Ruiz el Mozo.

The Cathedral

The fabulous treasures brought back from the New World financed the building of this remarkable temple with a rectangular groundplan (116 m long x 76 m wide x 56 m high) with five naves and around thirty chapels. Great Spanish, German and Flemish architects and artists took part in the construction of arches, stained-glass windows and carvings, such as those on the *Puerta de las Campanillas*, located between the Chapter House and the Royal Chapel, where the tombs of Fernando III "The Saint", Alfonso X "The Wise " and Pedro I "The Cruel" are located.

The Cathedral

Cristo de la Clemencia is one of the greatest artistic treasures of Seville Cathedral. This elegant and perfect carving is in the *Sacristía de los Cálices*, and is a masterpiece of Spanish Baroque. Its author, Juan Martínez Montañés, died a victim of the plague which struck the city in 1649.

The Chapter House, featuring a square groundplan and a superb dome with rose windows built by Hernán Ruiz II, houses the remains of Fernando III, which are inside a magnificent lavishly-carved silver coffin, work of 18th –century Sevillian silversmiths.

Este es Jesús Nazareno, Rey de los Judíos

זה ישוע נצרי מלך יהודם
ΟΥΤΟΣ ΕΣΤΙΝ ΙΗΣ ΝΑΖΩΡ Ο ΒΑΣΙΛ ΤΩΝ ΙΟΥΔΑΙΩΝ
HIC EST IES NAZAR REX IVDÆORVM

The Cathedral

The Patio de los Naranjos, along with the *Puerta del Perdón*, the *Puerta del Lagarto* and the *Giralda*, is a vestige of the ancient mosque built by the Almohades in the 12th century. This old courtyard is where the Muslims used to perform their ritual ablutions and is entered through the *Puerta del Perdón* and *Puerta de los Naranjos*. It owes its name to the orange trees which are symmetrically distributed through-out the courtyard, thus enhancing the harmony and tranquillity of the place.

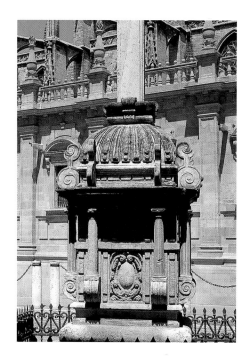

The monumentality and architectural richness of the Cathedral are extraordinary from the outside. Its walls, doors, for example those known as *Puerta del Perdón*, *Puerta del Nacimiento*, *Puerta de la Lonja*, *Oriente and Campanillas*, domes, *Giralda* bell tower and the rich ornamentation, all reveal the harmonic transit from Gothic to Neo-classical. This Cathedral is also one of the greatest monuments of Christian faith.

The Cathedral

Pilate's House

The Medinaceli Palace was known as "Pilate's House", according to some because Fadrique continued its construction in the style of Pontius Pilate's house when he came back from the Holy Land in 1521. Others believe it is due to the fact that it was here that the procession started during Holy Week. Columns, statues and busts like those of Janus and Vespasian, along with its refined orientalism, have always fostered popular legends.

Pilate's House

Mudéjar and Renaissance blend together in the sumptuous palace of the Medinaceli family. Its splendid patio combines perfect Roman columns and Mudéjar-style arches, whose lines enhance the adornment of wrought iron and tiles made by Sevillian artisans, a testimony of one of the most brilliant moments of Andalu-. sian Renaissance decorative arts.

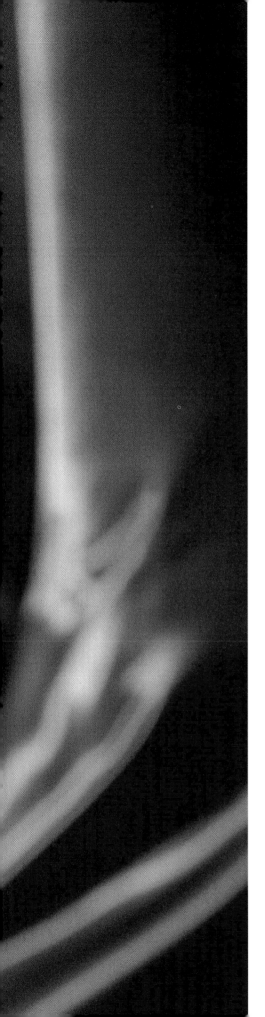

Holy Week

Religious fervour and solemnity, as well as pomp, prevail in the celebrations of Holy Week in Seville, whose intensity and colour are certainly unbeatable. From Palm Sunday to Good Friday numerous processions take place in the morning, afternoon and evening. Dozens of brotherhoods carry *pasos* (floats) through different streets depicting the stages of the Passion of Christ or of the Virgin, followed by penitent processioners dressed in their typical pointed hoods.

Streets and balconies are decked out and seating arranged for watching the processions go by. Thousands of people flock to Seville during Holy Week, drawn here by their religious piety and/or the beauty of the celebrations, whose most moving moments are when the *pasos* leave or enter their respective churches. But, apart from these demonstrations of faith, the Sevillians' sense of fun is also expressed, as well as their deep conviction that the Resurrection of Christ symbolises the triumph of life over death.

Holy Week

Holy Week

Saetas are spontaneously sung by anonymous admirers as the images go by, so expressing their faith and admiration, not without certain fervour and delirium. Each brotherhood usually accompanies two floats. The first one is usually a Christ on the Cross (to the right, *El Cachorro*) or a scene corresponding to the Passion, and the second, a *Mater Dolorosa* closing the procession. The first itinerary of the brotherhoods was established in 1520, between the chapel of *Pilate's House* and the *Cruz del Campo* Church. Now, there are nearly 50 different brotherhoods who take part in numerous processions.

Holy Week

Early on Good Friday morning, when the Virgin of the Macarena leaves her church, a profound emotion fills the streets of Seville. *Saetas* are intoned with deep sentiment and people break out in thunderous applause as the holy image solemnly passes by.

Urban Landscape

Town Hall. Impressive Plateresque construction built in1527 by Diego de Riaño, it is one of the most representative buildings of Sevillian civil architecture. Its elegant façade overlooks the *Plaza de San Francisco*, neuralgic centre in 16th –century Seville. Also ending up in this square is, for example, is the *Calle Sierpes*, a popular street where the famous and historical *La Campana* Confectioner's is located.

Urban Landscape

Archbishop's Palace. This 18th –century monumental Baroque building, standing in the *Plaza Virgen de los Reyes*, in front of the *Giralda* and the Cathedral, impresses us with its fountains, its tremendous marble staircase, the frescos on its walls and its museum which houses works by the best Spanish artists of the Renaissance.

Hospital de la Caridad. Devoted to looking after the poor, this magnificent Baroque building was erected following the orders of the somewhat tormented Miguel de Mañara, whose excesses, according to some, inspired the creation of *Don Juan Tenorio* by Tirso de Molina.

Urban Landscape

Royal Tobacco Factory. This building, now the University, is, together with *El Escorial*, the largest historical building in Spain. Built according to Neo-classical canons, with a splendid Baroque portal, it was formerly a cigarette factory where approximately 10,000 people worked. It was one of those cigarette makers who inspired Merimée's *Carmen*.

Museum of Fine Arts. The old medieval convent of the Order of the *Merced Calzada*, remodelled in a Renaissance style in the 17th century, houses the second largest pinacotheca in Spain.

Ŀa

Urban Landscape

Plaza de España. Centre of the 1929 Ibero-American Exhibition. Now a public park consisting of a large pond surrounded by a semi-elliptical building and a gallery of columns whose walls are covered in polychrome tiles featuring symbols and the history of the provinces of Spain.

(To the right and on the next two pages.)

Parks and Gardens

María Luisa Park

In 1893, the gardens of _San Telmo Palace_ were handed over to the city of Seville by _Infanta María Luisa de Orleans_ to be turned into a public park. It was later reordered in 1929. The _Glorieta de Bécquer_, the _Plaza de América_ and the 1929 Renaissance Pavilion are all part of this romantic space.

Parks and Gardens

Fountains, flower beds and trees are features of the *María Luisa Park*. The spirit of romance can be felt and seen in its "Fountain of the Lions" and small squares (*glorietas*) which are dedicated to Sevillian poets, including Gustavo Adolfo Bécquer, one of the greatest of the Spanish Romantics, and Antonio and Manuel Machado, whose verses express the innermost feelings of the soul.

Trees, fountains and flights of steps make up the harmonious layout of a park in motion. Tree branches and the arches formed by jets of water seem to play a game of contrasting light and shade. People constantly come and go along the quiet paths, through the cool shades and amid the colours, accompanied all the time by the sound of running water; others find a quiet place to rest beside the fountains.

The intense colours of the vegetation in *María Luisa Park* are an exaltation of Nature, light and colour; a tribute to the joy of living.

The delicate wrought ironwork of Sevillian blacksmiths imitates, just like Islamic art, plant shapes and contours. They are magnificent artistic creations which express and identify the close relationship between the human soul and Nature.

Parks and Gardens

Buildings with brick façades, which preserve their historical interest, seem to play hide-and-seek amidst the foliage. The abundant vegetation also indicates where we can stop and rest to get away from the hustle and bustle of city life.

Parks and Gardens

Murillo Gardens. Adjoining the gardens of the *Reales Alcázares*, and on one side of the impressive old *Tobacco Factory*, we can find the *Jardines de Murillo*, whose symmetry enhances the monument to Christopher Columbus. Very near here, almost in the district of *Santa Cruz*, lived Bartolomé Esteban Murillo, one of the main representatives of Spanish Baroque painting, together with Francisco Zurbarán, Juan de Valdés Leal and Alonso Cano.

The cross known as Cruz de la Cerrajería, looms up from behind the trees of the *Plaza de Santa Cruz* ("Square of the Holy Cross"), in the district of *Santa Cruz*. This Christian symbol made of splendid wrought iron has given the popular neighbourhood its name, being a landmark of the district, whose white houses and narrow streets make up an urban maze. The *Barrio de Santa Cruz* was formerly the Jewish quarter of the city and still maintains an ambience of Bohemian magic.

Peaceful, sunny patios behind beautiful wrought-iron gates, which allow us to admire the polychrome tiles adorning their walls, the pots of flowers, a fountain or a small garden. An intelligent synthesis between Roman *villas* and Muslim tradition can be seen in the typical Andalusian layout of the *Barrio de Santa Cruz*. An urban space characterised by its narrow, labyrinthine streets, where pleasant surprises constantly await us.

White, luminous or brightly-coloured houses make up the urban landscape of the typical *Sevillian Barrio de Santa Cruz*, neuralgic centre of the old part of the city. Formerly the old Jewish quarter, its layout is an intricate maze of narrow streets with evocative and drastic names such as *Muerte y Vida* ("Death and Life"), and others like *Pimienta* ("Pepper"), *del Moro* ("The Moor's) or *del Agua* ("The Water"). In the *Plaza de Doña Elvira*, formerly a playhouse, stands today the Hospital de *Venerables Sacerdotes*, old residence for retired priests, which has a beautiful chapel decorated by Juan and Lucas Valdés, as well as a splendid patio.

Parks and Gardens

Along the Guadalquivir

The River Guadalquivir, called Wadi el Kebir ("great river") by the Arabs and then *Betis* by the Romans, has always been (and still is) the artery of Seville. Spanning it are the old bridges of *Isabel II* or *Triana* (seen below) or the modern ones of *La Barqueta* and *El Alamillo* (left and above).

The celebration of the 1992 World Exhibition was decisive for the urban development and modernisation of Seville. The choice of the *Isla de la Cartuja* meant the recovery of an original space in the middle of the River Guadalquivir, which has given the urban landscape a futuristic look. The Finland Pavilion, today the head office of the Seville College of Architects, is a fine example of this.

Along the

Auditorium. The *Cartuja de Santa María de las Cuevas* was a medieval monastery; it was here that Christopher Columbus lived, worked and was buried -in the Chapel of *Santa Ana*. In the 19th century, Charles Pickman founded a famous ceramics factory here. Impressive constructions have been built in this area, such as this auditorium.

Guadalquivir

The calm waters of the Guadalquivir and the lush vegetation along its banks enhance the urban landscape of Seville. The murmur of the river and the fragrance of flowers are a paradise for the city. A lively city full of fun, where a rich historic past lives alongside a dynamic present, which has known how to adjust to the rhythm of the future. Gracious Seville and the calm Guadalquivir that never rest.

The sturdy and elegant Torre del Oro ("Tower of Gold") stands out on the riverside. Built in the 13th century by the Almohades as part of the *Alcázar's* defence system, this 12-sided tower used to be covered in golden tiles and was communicated with another tower known as "Tower of Silver" (now vanished). These two towers were where the gold and silver coming from America were kept until the *Casa de la Contratación* was created.

Along the Guadalquivir

Feria de Abril

An explosion of merriment and colour, the "April Fair" is one of the celebrations which best defines the character of Seville. A fortnight after Easter Sunday, the Sevillians fill the streets to celebrate an internationally-famous event. Thousands of visitors come here every year, eager to take part in the great *fiesta*, and mix with riders, horse-drawn carriages and people who sing and dance to the sound of tambours accompanied by rhythmic hand-clapping.

All dressed up in typical costumes, Sevillians parade around the fairgrounds of the *Remedios* District, and the whole city oozes happiness. According to some, this *feria* has its origins in the unification of two agricultural fairs known as *Cincuesma* and *San Miguel* by King Alfonso X in 1292. However, the nearest historical reference dates back to 1847, when Queen Isabel II renewed the learned king's decree and three years later approved the separation of the livestock market and the farmers' recreational area. Even so, the Fair did not acquire its current layout until the third decade of the 20th century.

Feria de Abril

During the April Fair coloured garlands stand out against the blue sky, representing the festive and merry spirit prevailing in Seville during a long, intense week of celebrations.

Feria de Abril

Pretty girls dressed in short jackets and wide-brimmed hats parade around the fairground mounted on fiery horses just like the men. The latter are accompanied by women riding pillion wearing typical frilly, polka-dotted dresses, a shawl round their shoulders, and flowers in their hair or on their breast, whilst families do so in luxurious horse-drawn carriages.

Colourful pavilions and columns adorned with flowers and paper lanterns decorate the fairgrounds, although the whole city is merrymaking, heel-tapping, hand-clapping, flamenco singing, *sevillana* dancing, food and wine.

(See next two pages.)

The Maestranza

The Maestranza Bullring is perhaps the most emblematic one in Spain. Important bullfights are held in this "temple of bullfighting" even during Holy Week, the April Fair and the *San Miguel* Fair. Fine bullfighters' costumes and images of famous bullfighters can be seen in the *Museum of Bullfighting* that is housed inside.

SOMBRA
BARRERAS
TENDIDOS 2-4-6

Seville's famous bullring, La Maestranza was built between 1761 and 1881 at the request of the *San Hermenegildo* equestrian society of Spanish noblemen (*La Maestranza* in Spanish.) Bullfights have been held in Seville since medieval days, when knights used to show off their skills to the masses by spearing wild bulls. These celebrations were paid for by nobles or by the Council and were usually held at the same time as important civil or religious events.

The Maestranza